GREETINGS FROM SWARTSWOOD
Volume #2

Old Mill and High Falls, Swartswood, N. J.

Postcards from the Lake

SCOTT M. GORISCAK

SWARTSWOOD PUBLICATIONS
2024

I dedicate this book to my children. I love you all.

Thank you to the Tosti Family, Mr, & Mrs. Michael Skinner, Mr. & Mrs. Chris Welles, Mr. and Mrs. Andy Martin, Mr. & Mrs. Peter Mahler, Mr. & Mrs. Steven Meng, Ms. Joan Larenzo, and Mr. & Mrs. Bob Goehring for all the wonderful contributions and historical conversations about Swartswood.

ISBN: 9798326720009

INTRODUCTION

Hello, and welcome to Swartswood, New Jersey! It was not too long ago, when I heard that Swartswood was approaching its bicentennial.(2024) I took a moment and reflected about this and realized that after living here for the past thirty years, I knew little about our village's history. This is where my historical curiosity got the best of me. I started researching Swartswood on the internet, at libraries, and speaking to local folks and members of our historical society. I quickly discovered endless facts and events about our town, the settlers, and the indians! Most of the history was scattered about, there was no real source that brought it all together. After six months of research I decided to document my findings about our town. There was by no means any shortage of material, however, I was not looking to write a six hundred page history book, my goal was to write a book that would introduce readers to our village and it's historical past in a friendly simple manner. The only way I would be able to do this was to break up the information into multiple volumes. "Greetings from Swartswood" will be my first book about Swartswood, NJ. Book one is a collection of postcards of the town and the lake. What I love about this book is the many postcards I was fortunate to locate had personal messages from the sender to loved ones and friends. It seems that Swartswood was not a quiet sleepy town as it appears today. Families and friends around the turn of the century chose Swartswood as their destination for fun and relaxation. Family vacations, weekend getaways and fishing trips populated Swartswood lake year round. Please enjoy this trip down memory lane as you read through the postcards of Swartswood visitors past and reminisce of days gone by. I hope you enjoy this photograhic journey of yesterday as much as I had discovering it for myself.

Scott

Road to Swartswood, Newton, N. J.

The Old Spring, Swartswood Lake, Middleville, N. J. 17,179

Picturesque Railroad Hill, on drive from Newton to Swartswood, N. J.

MONTE ALLEGRO—COMPLETE REST
& RELAXATION SWARTSWOOD, N.J.
Tel. Newton 939 F14

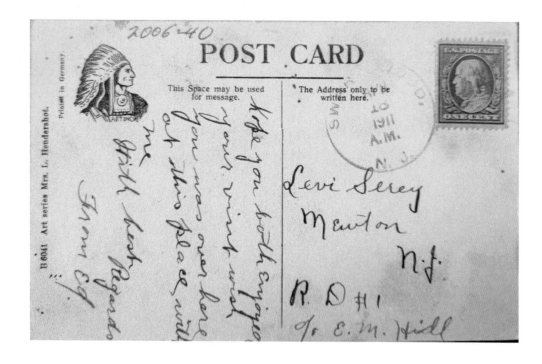

VIEW ON SWARTSWOOD ROAD

Dear Byron, - this is a picture of the dam of Mr. Morris's mill pond. There is a boat on the pond and we have a good time now. Love to Papa & Mama. Aunt Dora.

Oct. 4, 1906.

POST Card

Master C Byron Blaisdell,
Norwood Avenue,
Long Branch,
N. J.

(Sta. B.)

Cinsworn.

VIEW ON SWARTSWOOD ROAD

Your Friend Cornie

Dear may
I suppose
you go to
school
every day
How are
you by
this time

Excuse my writing because Because
it is awful poor will write better next ai

GUIRRERI'S FIVE POINTS INN, R. D. No. 2, NEWTON, N. J.

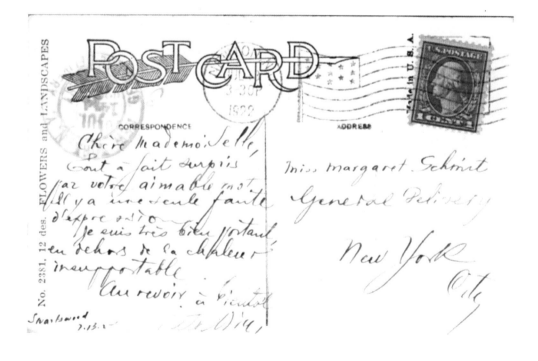

Guerreri's Five Point Inn   Newton, N. J.

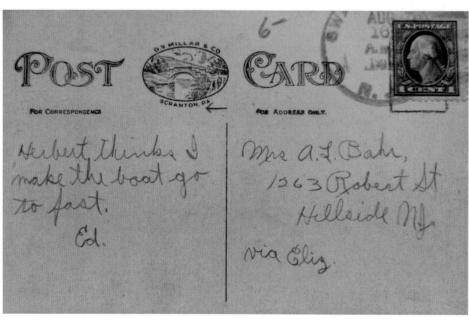

POST CARD

G.V. MILLAR & CO
SCRANTON, PA.

FOR CORRESPONDENCE

FOR ADDRESS ONLY.

Herbert thinks I
make the boat go
to fast.
    Ed.

Mrs A. L. Bahr,
1563 Robert St
Hillside N.J.

via Eliz.

M. M. BUNN, LAKESIDE HOUSE, SWARTSWOOD N. J.

View from near Lakeview House, Swartswood Lake,
Middleville, N. J.

16011

Bunn's Boat Landing, SWARTSWOOD LAKE, N. J.

BUNN'S COVE, SWARTSWOOD LAKE, N. J.

"THE PINES," SWARTSWOOD LAKE, N. J.   Elmer E. Hill, Prop.

"THE PINES," Elmer Hill, Prop.   Swartswood Lake, N. J.

CLUB CASINO, SWARTSWOOD LAKE, MIDDLEVILLE, N. J.

WEST SHORE LODGE. HAROLD & LENA MASSA. HOTEL — bar
RESTAURANT. PHONE, NEWTON 9436 ON SWARTSWOOD

TERRACE VIEW, CLUB CASINO (WEST SHORE), SWARTSWOOD LAKE, N. J.

THE PROMENADE, CLUB CASINO—WEST SHORE—SWARTSWOOD LAKE, N. J.

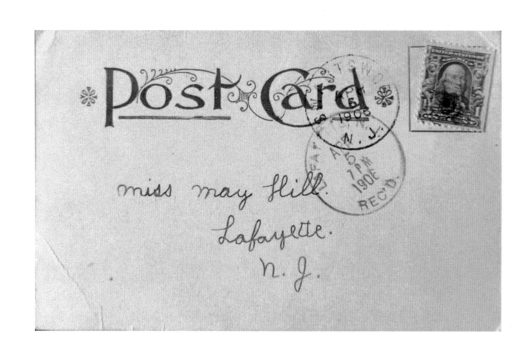

POST CARD

miss may Hill.
Lafayette.
n. J.

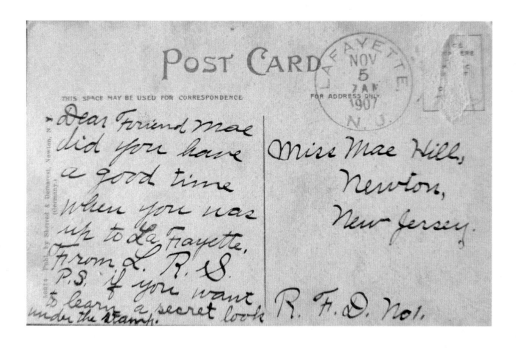

POST CARD

THIS SPACE MAY BE USED FOR CORRESPONDENCE

FOR ADDRESS ONLY

LAFAYETTE
NOV
5
7 AM
1907
N. J.

Dear Friend Mae
did you have
a good time
when you was
up to LaFayette.
from L. R. S.
P. S. if you want
to learn a secret look
under the stamp.

Miss Mae Hill,
Newton,
New Jersey.

R. F. D. No. 1.

POST CARD

Dear friends

I am here staying
a few days with
Mrs. Buckman.
We are going down
to Asbury this
Saturday Sun. will
let you know when
I come back
H. Weise

Mr & Mrs. Hebach
57 Adams Place
Glen Ridge
N. J.

PUBLISHED BY SHERRED'S BUSY STORE, NEWTON, N. J.

Post Cards of Quality. — The Albertype Co., Brooklyn, N.Y.

THIS SPACE FOR MESSAGE

THIS SPACE FOR ADDRESS

DR. RICE'S AT HIGH FALLS. SWARTSWOOD, N. J.

HIGH FALLS, SWARTSWOOD, N. J.

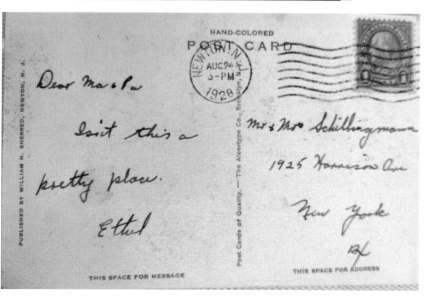

HAND-COLORED
POST CARD

Dear Ma & Pa

Isn't this a

pretty place.

Ethel

PUBLISHED BY WILLIAM H. SHERRED, NEWTON, N. J.

Post Cards of Quality.—The Albertype Co., Brooklyn, N. Y.

Mr & Mrs Schillingmann

1925 Harrison Ave

New York

THIS SPACE FOR MESSAGE

THIS SPACE FOR ADDRESS

High Falls, Swartswood Lake, N. J.

AT THE OLD MILL.
RESIDENCE OF DR. C. C. RICE.
NEAR NEWTON, N. J.

POST CARD

THIS SPACE MAY BE USED FOR CORRESPONDENCE

address High Falls House
Swartswood, N. J.
We haven't forgotten you
Jack is here for two
weeks, and I think
Gordon and I will stay
about four. We are eight
miles from Newton.
The cross marks the house
where we are staying.
How are you all? I often
think of you, but when
I am home I can't find time
to do more than think of my
friends. Sue N. J.

SWARTSWOOD
N. J.
JUL 29
1908

Mrs. Frank Whitehead,
57 Harrison St.,
Rahway.
N. J.

AT THE OLD MILL.
RESIDENCE OF DR. C. C. RICE.
NEAR NEWTON, N. J.

High Falls House, Swartswood, N. J.

High Falls House

HIGH FALLS   SWARTSWOOD, N. J.

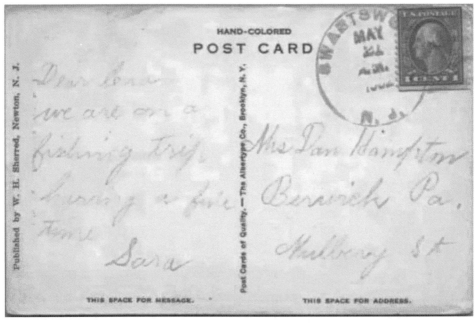

HAND-COLORED
POST CARD

THIS SPACE FOR MESSAGE.   THIS SPACE FOR ADDRESS.

ENTRANCE TO JUDGE LAWRENCE'S BUNGALOW AND LITTLE SWARTSWOOD LAKE. N. J.

Lawrence's Bungalow
Swartswood Lake N.J.

SWARTSWOOD LAKE, N. J.; SHOWING JUDGE LAWRENCE'S BUNGALOW
ON THE NEWTON — SWARTSWOOD ROAD.

Bietz's Bungalow   Swartswood Lake, N. J.

SWARTSWOOD LAKE, N.J.

POST CARD

THIS SPACE MAY BE USED FOR CORRESPONDENCE

FOR ADDRESS ONLY.

Bin hier seit den 4 den diesen Monat Alle wohl.

Mrs. F. M. Manger Jr.

Mr. & Mrs

Sommer

191½ North Street

Jersey City

N.J.

Pub. by William H. Nichols, Newton, N.J. (Germany.)

MILL POND. SWARTSWOOD.
NEAR NEWTON. N. J.

MILL POND. SWARTSWOOD. MIDDLEVILLE. N. J.

Keene's Mill, Swartswood, N.J.

When you come up
Sunday will you
please bring my
toothbrush its on
the shelf above the
sink and Elsie's pin
for the back of her
neck on the stand in
our room Estella

Mr. Milton Southard
Middleville
N. J.

No. 1517. Publ by International Post Card Co. New York. 3. Made in Germany

Mill Dam Keen's Mill, Middleville, N. J.

View from Keens, SWARTSWOOD LAKE, N. J.

OLD GRIST MILL, Swartswood, N. J.

We all want to know Monday if you arrived home ok. Arthur

Keen's Mill, Swartswood Lake,
MIDDLEVILLE, N. J.

THE FOREBAY, SWARTSWOOD LAKE, MIDDLEVILLE, N.J.

THE MILLDAM, SWARTSWOOD LAKE, MIDDLEVILLE, N.J.

Wednesday.
Dear R.E.
I guess I have told
Tant so all the news.
We were in bathing in
the A.M. and had a
row on the lake, after
dinner we listened to
the phonograph and
then I had a drive to
Middleville at night
we were all to the kittens
who had a party of 10
fellows visiting them.

They started to camp but the mosquitoes proved too much and they
slept here the rest of the week. To-night we are going to leave some
people to spend the evening among them the 10 boys, expect a good time.

We have just had a "Manhattan"
so you know how we feel and
had we are behaving. We
had a nice meal with respect
for what ails us; wish you could
join us.   Sincerely   MaJane

THE WHITE SWANS
Middleville, Sussex County, New Jersey

POST CARD

Address

PLACE
STAMP
HERE

Mr Carl Roof
Star Route
Woodstock, Vt
05091

Scene near Swartswood, Sussex Co., N. J.

$40

POST CARD

VELOX
PLACE
STAMP
HERE
VELOX

CORRESPONDENCE HERE

NAME AND ADDRESS HERE

Swartswood N.J.
July 7th 1911
The weather is terrible
hot and dry all over
this part of the country.
Hope you are more com-
fortable - had lots of company
and kept busy will write
soon.

Mrs A. P. Meres
Tarpon Spgs
Fla

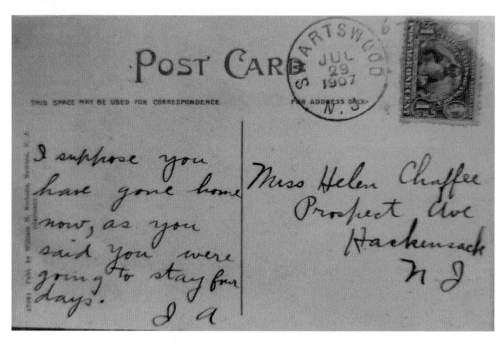

Mr. Pratt drove me here yesterday (Tues.) We had a delightful drive of 30 miles. Started 15 to 10 o'clock and got home 8 o'clock. Earle

THE COTTAGE. SWARTSWOOD LAKE. MIDDLEVILLE. N.J.

A. ROBBINS & Son

You can look for a letter soon.

POST CARD

THIS SPACE MAY BE USED FOR CORRESPONDENCE.

FOR ADDRESS ONLY.

SWARTSWOOD JUL 29 1907 N.J.

I suppose you have gone home now, as you said you were going to stay four days.
J a

Miss Helen Chaffee
Prospect Ave
Hackensack
N J

VIEW FROM THE GREENWOODS.
SWARTSWOOD LAKE. MIDDLEVILLE. N. J.

POST CARD

THIS SPACE MAY BE USED FOR CORRESPONDENCE   FOR ADDRESS ONLY

Miss Anna Giordano,

Newton,

New Jersey

Greenwood Point, Swartswood Lake, N. J.

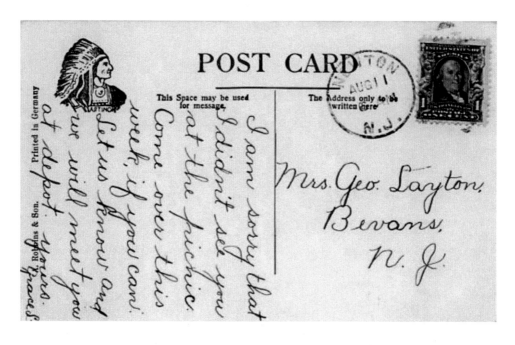

POST CARD

This Space may be used for message.

The Address only to be written here

I am sorry that I didn't see you at the picnic. Come over this week, if you can. Let us know and we will meet you at depot. Yours truly, Graces

Printed in Germany

W. Robbins & Son.

Mrs. Geo. Layton.
Bevans,
N. J.

GREENWOOD POINT,
MIDDLEVILLE, N.J.

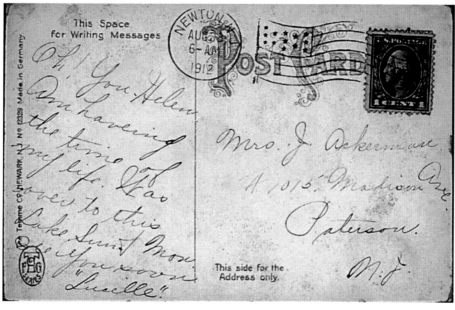

This Space
for Writing Messages

This side for the
Address only.

Oh! You Helen
Am having
the time of
my life. Has
over to this
Lake Sunt Mon
Yourown
"Lucille"

Mrs. J. Ackerman
1015. Madison Ave.
Paterson.
N.J.

John Emman's Boat House, Swartswood Lake, N. J.

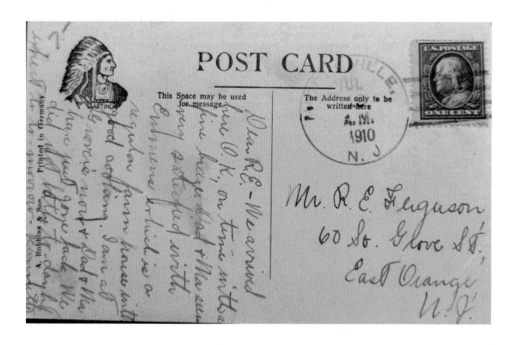

POST CARD

This Space may be used
for message.

The Address only to be
written here

Dear R.E - We arrived
here O.K., on time with the
fine house. Dad & Ma are
very satisfied with
Everything which is a
regular farm house with
a good setting. I am al-
together rich & Dad & Ma
have had one back We
died all getting day of
which we are ac-

Mr. R. E. Ferguson
60 So. Grove St,
East Orange
N. J

Boat House in Emman's Grove, Swartswood Lake, N. J.

Wintermute Mill, Middleville, N. J.

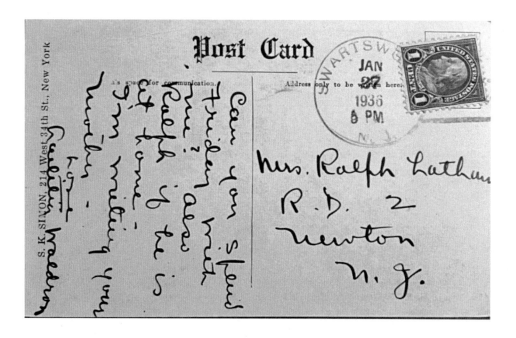

Post Card

This space for communication.

Address only to be written here.

SWARTSW
JAN
2?
1936
8 PM
N. J.

Can you spend
Friday with
me? also
Ralph if he is
at home —
I'm missing your
visits —
home
Guelita Waldron

Mrs. Ralph Latham
R. D. 2
Newton
N. J.

Mt. Brook House, Middleville, N. J.

Middleville Blacksmith Shop.

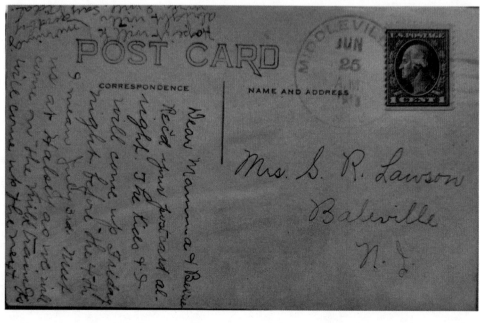

POST CARD

CORRESPONDENCE

NAME AND ADDRESS

MIDDLEVILLE
JUN
25

Mrs. S. R. Lawson
Baleville
N. J.

BATHING BEACH, SWARTSWOOD LAKE, N. J.

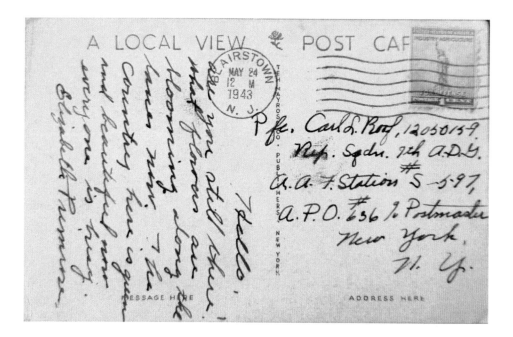

A LOCAL VIEW ❦ POST CARD

THE MAYROSE CO. PUBLISHERS. NEW YORK

BLAIRSTOWN
MAY 24
12 M
1943
N. J.

All you still there!
What flowers are
blooming along the
lanes now. The
Country here is green
and beautiful now—
everyone is busy.
Elizabeth Primrose.

Hello,

Pfc. Carl L. Roof, 12050159.
Rep. Sqdn. 9th A.D.G.
A. A. F. Station #5-97,
A. P. O. #636 ℅ Postmaster
New York,
N. Y.

MESSAGE HERE   ADDRESS HERE

Johnson's Cove, Swartswood Lake,
MIDDLEVILLE, N. J.

GRANNY'S POINT, SWARTSWOOD LAKE, N. J.

GRANNY'S POINT, SWARTSWOOD, N. J.

Camping, Swartswood Lake, Middleville, N. J.　17,178

Bathing Beach,
Swartswood Lake, N. J.

BUNN'S COVE, SWARTSWOOD LAKE, N. J.

POST CARD

NEWTON, N. J.
FEB 14
5-PM
1938

PUB. BY BEAUX ART PHOTO, TRENTON, N. J.

Feb. 9. 1938
Dear Sir.
Please sent
me one of your 1938
Spring & Summer Catalog
I would like to have one as
as so to get one of it for me.
Guin Florence Elder no
R.D.2. Newton N. J.

THIS SPACE FOR MESSAGE

The National Bellas Hess
New york City
New york

THIS SPACE FOR ADDRESS

Waldron's Landing,
Swartswood Lake, N.J.

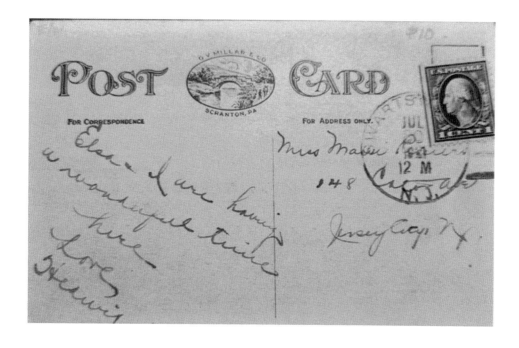

POST CARD

G.V. MILLAR & CO.
SCRANTON, PA.

FOR CORRESPONDENCE   FOR ADDRESS ONLY.

Elsa — I are having
a wonderful time
here
Love
Irwin

Mrs Maker Pavier
148

Jersey City N.Y.

(Pub. by V. M. Robbins)

WALDRON'S, SWARTSWOOD LAKE, MIDDLEVILLE, N. J.

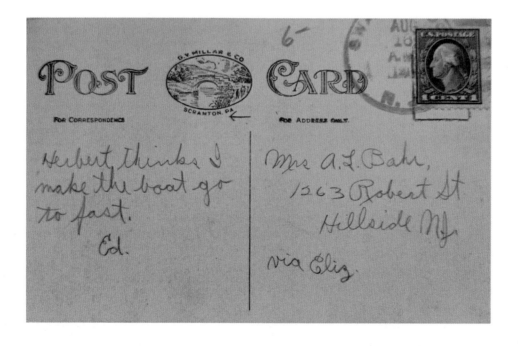

POST CARD

G. V. MILLAR & CO
SCRANTON, PA.

FOR CORRESPONDENCE

FOR ADDRESS ONLY.

Herbert thinks I
make the boat go
to fast.
    Ed.

Mrs A. L. Bahr,
1263 Robert St
Hillside N J

via Eliz.

SWARTSWOOD LAKE NEAR NEWTON, N. J.

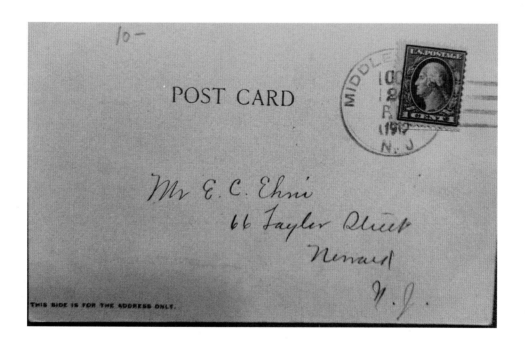

10-

POST CARD

Mr E. C. Ehni
66 Tayler Street
Neward
N. J.

Echo Lake, Stillwater, N. J.

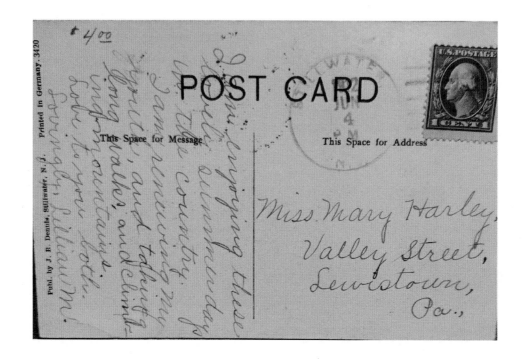

POST CARD

This Space for Message

This Space for Address

Printed in Germany. 3420

Publ. by J. R. Denise, Stillwater, N. J.

Miss Mary Harley,
Valley Street,
Lewistown,
Pa.,

The Cottages, SWARTSWOOD LAKE, N. J.

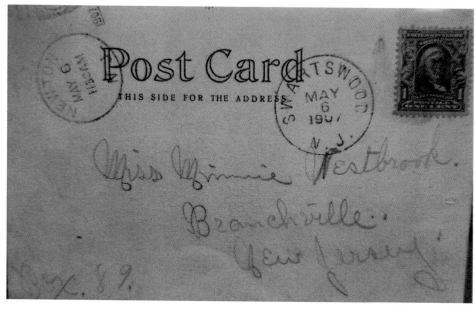

Post Card

THIS SIDE FOR THE ADDRESS

Miss Minnie Westbrook.
Branchville.
New Jersey

Box. 89.

REFRESHMENT PAVILLION, SWARTSWOOD STATE PARK, SWARTSWOOD LAKE, N. J.

PICNIC GROVE, SWARTSWOOD STATE PARK, SWARTSWOOD LAKE, N. J.

SAND BEACH AT SWARTSWOOD STATE PARK, SWARTSWOOD LAKE, N. J.

PUB. BY A. MORRIS, STATE PARK, SWARTSWOOD LAKE, N. J.

PHOTO-TONE
POST CARD

Eagle Post Card View Co., inc., New York

BATHING BEACH   SWARTSWOOD LAKE, N. J.

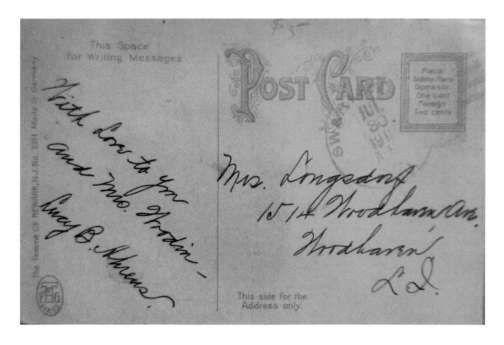

This Space
for Writing Messages

With love to you
and Mr. Hardin.

Lucy B. Ahrens

POST CARD

Place
Stamp Here
Domestic
One cent
Foreign
Two cents

This side for the
Address only.

Mrs. Longdorf
1514 Woodlawn Av.
Woodhaven
L. I.

Bathing Beach, Swartswood Lake, N. J.

BATHING DOCK, SWARTSWOOD STATE PARK, SWARTSWOOD LAKE, N. J.

Swartswood Lake, N. J.

SWARTSWOOD LAKE, N. J.

Hill View
Swartswood Lake, N. J.

10977

SWARTSWOOD LAKE, N. J.

Greetings from SWARTSWOOD, NEW JERSEY

Summer Guests, Swartswood Lake, N. J.

Swartswood Lake, near NEWTON, N. J.

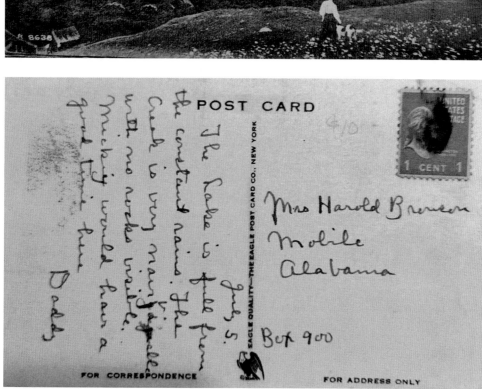

POST CARD

EAGLE QUALITY—THE EAGLE POST CARD CO., NEW YORK

July 5.

The Lake is full from
the constant rains. The
Creek is very manageable
with no rocks visible.
Mickey would have a
good time here

Daddy

Mrs Harold Bronson
Mobile
Alabama

Box 900

FOR CORRESPONDENCE

FOR ADDRESS ONLY

UNITED STATES POSTAGE
1 CENT 1

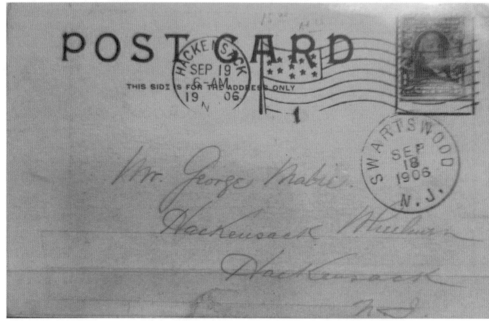

POST CARD

THIS SIDE IS FOR THE ADDRESS ONLY

THE NARROWS, SWARTSWOOD LAKE, MIDDLEVILLE, N. J. (Pub. by V. M. Robbins)

Hello Ed
Bring your
camera along
with you Sunday
I want to use
it
So long from Nataly

Mr. Ed Bowman
Long Valley
N J.
R D #1

PUBLISHED BY W. H. SHERRED, NEWTON, N. J.

Post Cards of Quality.—The Albertype Co., Brooklyn, N. Y.

HAND COLORED
POST CARD

MAY 28 1932

c o Frank Bowman

GREETINGS FROM SWARTSWOOD, N. J.

A Cozy Nook, Swartswood Lake, Middleville, N. J.

Swartswood Lake.

POST CARD

Pub. by Wm. H. Nichols, Newton, N. J.

NEWTON, N
JUL 30
1 - PM
1928

50c

Mrs. G C Bowmann

429 Ave O,

Brooklyn,

New York

7/30/28

Cozy Nook, Swartswood. N. J.

POST CARD

NEWTON, N. J.
FEB 14
5-PM
1938

Pub. by BEAUX ART PHOTO, TUCKPORT

THIS SPACE FOR MESSAGE

Feb 9, 1938

Dear Sir.

Please send
me one of your 1938
Spring & Summer Catalog
I like to have one I
like to get one photo from
you Florence Stiger
RD2, Newton N.J.

The National Bellas Hess

New York City

New York

THIS SPACE FOR ADDRESS

SWARTSWOOD LAKE, N. J.

(Pub. by V. M. Robbins)

HILLTOP VIEW OF SWARTSWOOD LAKE, MIDDLEVILLE, N. J.

Swartswood Lake, N. J.

Swartswood Lake, N. J.

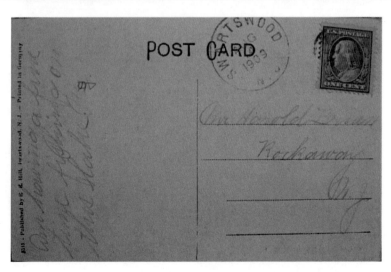

17394 Lisis where Dr. plays.

LOTUS LANDING.
Swartswood Lake, N. J.

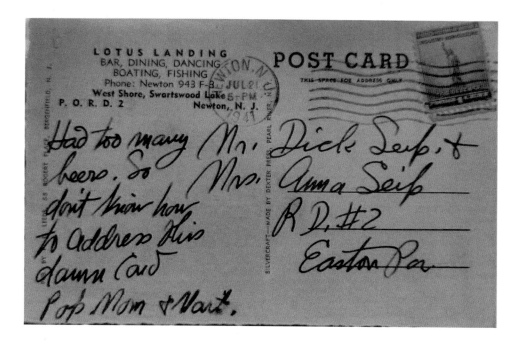

LOTUS LANDING
BAR, DINING, DANCING
BOATING, FISHING
Phone: Newton 943 F-3
West Shore, Swartswood Lake
P. O. R. D. 2   Newton, N. J.

POST CARD
THIS SPACE FOR ADDRESS ONLY

Had too many
beers. So
don't know how
to address this
damn card
Pop Mom & Nart.

Mr.
Mrs.

Dick Seip, &
Anna Seip
R D. #2
Easton Pa.

SCENIC DRIVE FROM NEWTON TO SWARTSWOOD LAKE, N. J.

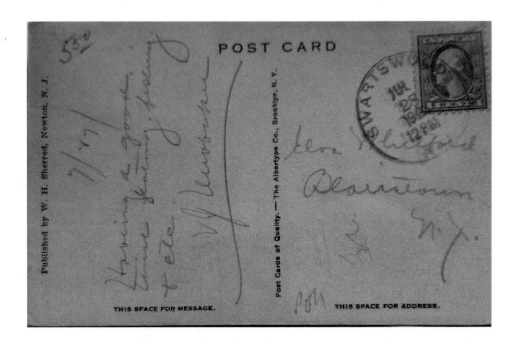

POST CARD

Published by W. H. Sherred, Newton, N. J.

THIS SPACE FOR MESSAGE.

Post Cards of Quality. — The Albertype Co., Brooklyn, N. Y.

THIS SPACE FOR ADDRESS.

PAULINS KILL, SWARTSWOOD, N. J.

CLUB HOUSE, DAM AND BEACH
Paulinskill Lake, N. J.

POST OFFICE & GENERAL STORE, SWARTSWOOD, N.J.

THE POST OFFICE, SWARTSWOOD, N.J.

DOVE ISLAND COLONY, SWARTSWOOD LAKE, NEWTON, N. J.
THE BOAT DOCK

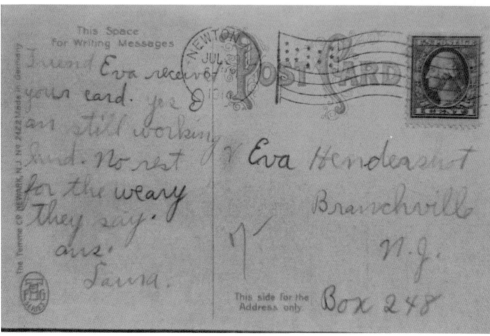

This Space
For Writing Messages

Friend Eva received
your card. yes I
am still working
hard. No rest
for the weary
they say.
ans.
Laura.

NEWTON
JUL
1912

POST CARD

Eva Hendershot
Branchville
N. J.

This side for the
Address only

Box 248

CAMP ALONG LAKE, SWARTSWOOD STATE PARK, SWARTSWOOD LAKE, N. J.

Dove Island, Swartswood Lake - Dec. 1950

(Pub. by V. M. Robbins)

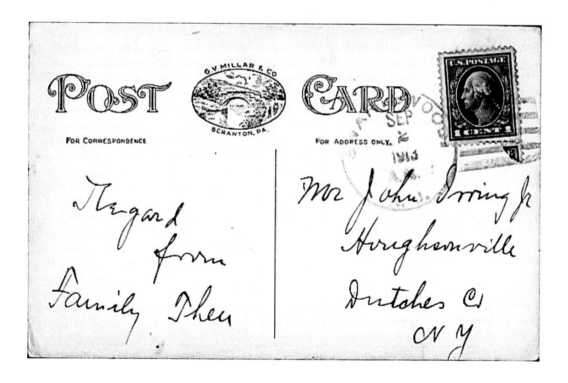

Regard
from
Family Theu

Mr John Irving Jr
Houghonville
Dutches C.
N Y

Dove Island, Swartswood Lake, N. J.

PHOTO-TONE
POST CARD

Fish House Ticket Studio

H'ya Edie,
        Got your a super-
dooper letter —
terrific! Blothin
up sun for a while
here—killing off the
insect population
by degrees, but I'll
show you my bite lamps
when I see you. Promise to get ambitious+

Miss E. Takaro
2920 160 STREET
Flushing
LONG Island

write love
letter Es

PUB. BY A. MORRIS, STATE PARK, SWARTSWOOD LAKE, N. J.

US POSTAGE

7.50

Dove Island Outlook, Swartswood Lake, N. J.   12334

DOVE ISLAND.   SWARTSWOOD LAKE, N. J.

POST CARD

GREENDELL
AUG
8
1921

Published by W. H. Sherred, Newton, N. J.

Post Cards of Quality.— The Albertype Co., Brooklyn, N. Y.

Here is the
boat. have you
the time?
X

Mrs Carrie De Roon
143 Main St
Paterson
n J

THIS SPACE FOR MESSAGE.

THIS SPACE FOR ADDRESS.

HILL'S NOOK.   SWARTSWOOD LAKE, N. J.

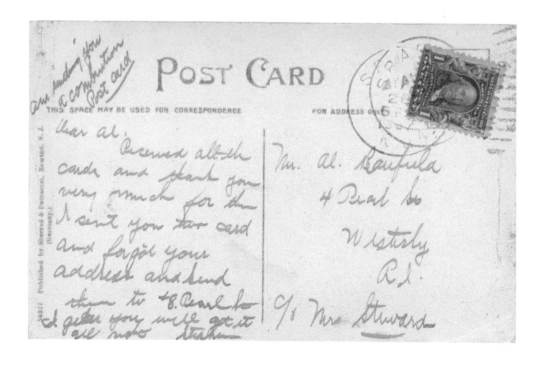

HILL'S CASINO. SWARTSWOOD LAKE. N. J.

HILL'S CASINO ON SWARTSWOOD LAKE, Swartswood, N. J.

A Big Happy Family at Kamp Kiamesha

Printed in Germany. B 6043 Art series Mrs. L. Hendershot.

POST CARD

This Space may be used
for message.

The Address only to be
written here.

PLACE
POSTAGE STAMP
HERE.

DOMESTIC
1 CENT.

FOREIGN
2 CENTS.

"Setting Up" Drill at Kamp Kiamesha,
an early morning scene

POST CARD

This side for Correspondence

Kamp Kiamesha in the Blue Ridge
Mountains of New Jersey, conducted by
Newark Y. M. C. A., N. J. Mail Address,
Swartswood, N. J.

Here is one of
things we have
to lifen us up
in the morning
before breakfast
Bennett

This side for Address.

Mrs. Paul Brangs
336 Roseville Ave
newark
n. J.

IN SWARTSWOOD LAKE, N. J.

Swartswood Lake. N. J.

Greetings from MIDDLEVILLE, N. J.

PEACEFUL SCENE   S-364

SWARTSWOOD LAKE, NEWTON, N. J.   3A-H1614

GREETINGS FROM SWARTSWOOD STATE PARK, N J

Greetings from MIDDLEVILLE, N. J.

12754

L-117

GREETINGS FROM SWARTSWOOD LAKE. N.J.

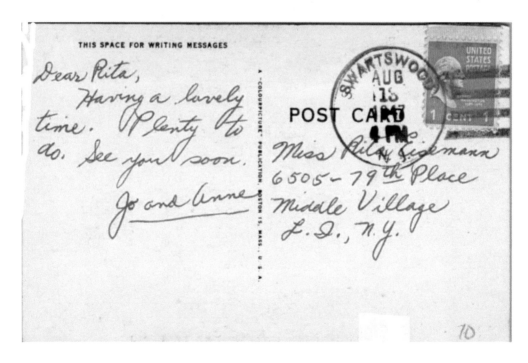

THIS SPACE FOR WRITING MESSAGES

Dear Rita,
        Having a lovely
time. Plenty to
do. See you soon.
            Jo and Anne

POST CARD

A "COLOURPICTURE" PUBLICATION. BOSTON 15, MASS., U. S. A.

Miss Rita Eisemann
6505 - 79th Place
Middle Village
L. I., N. Y.

A View of the Pond at
CAMP ALDERSGATE
Swartswood, New Jersey 07877

Northern New Jersey Conference
THE UNITED METHODIST CHURCH

Post Card

TRI-TRIBE BEACH
ROUTE 521   SWARTSWOOD, NEW JERSEY
FILTERED POOL — PICNIC AREA
RESTAURANT STAND — KIDDIE POOL
BOATING ON SWARTSWOOD LAKE

Tri-Tribe Beach is located on the shores of beautiful Swartswood Lake on the site of the historic Swartout property after which the lake was named.

American Aerial Survey Co., Hackettstown, N. J.

POST CARD
Address

35484

Greetings from **Swartswood Lake** NEW JERSEY

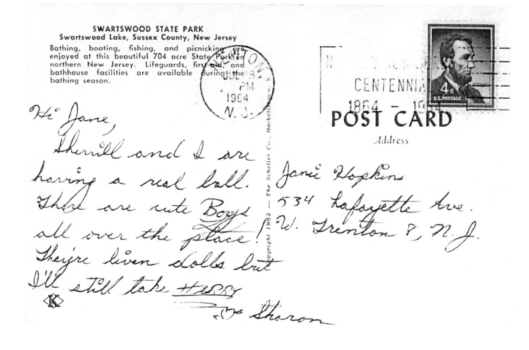

SWARTSWOOD STATE PARK
Swartswood Lake, Sussex County, New Jersey

Bathing, boating, fishing, and picnicking are
enjoyed at this beautiful 704 acre State Park in
northern New Jersey. Lifeguards, first-aid, and
bathhouse facilities are available during the
bathing season.

CENTENNIAL
1864 – 19
POST CARD
Address

4¢
U.S.POSTAGE

Hi Jane,
Sherrill and I are
having a real ball.
There are cute Boys
all over the place!
They're liven dolls but
I'll still take HARRY

Love Sharon

Jane Hopkins
534 Lafayette Ave.
W. Trenton 8, N. J.

Copyright 1962 — The Scheller Co., Hackettstown, N. J.

Thanks for visiting Swartswood, NJ.

8e70e8d5-e00f-4fed-ad23-40bad71acb5eR02